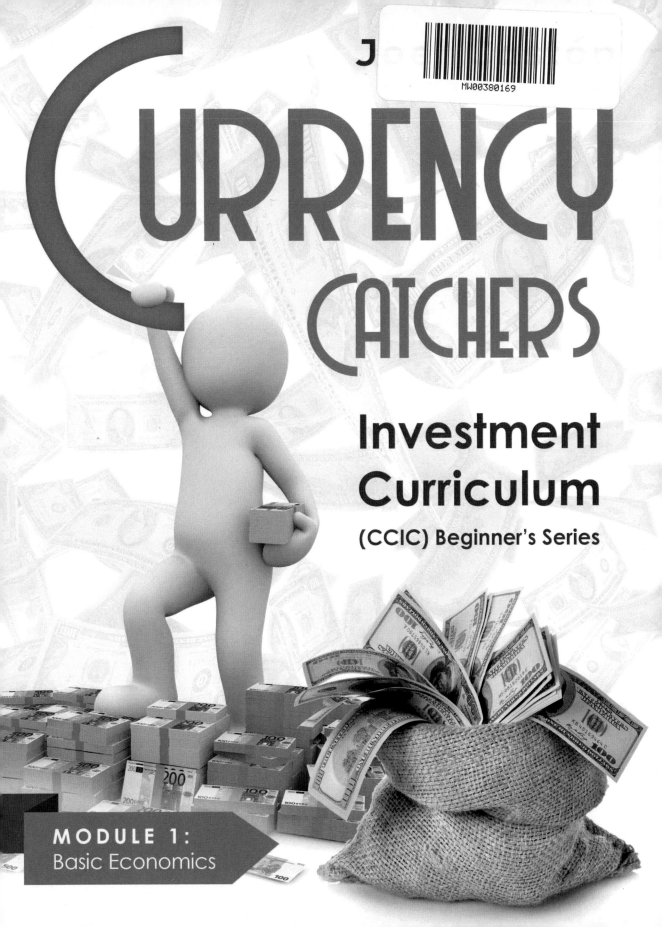

CURRENCY CATCHERS

Investment Curriculum

(CCIC) Beginner's Series

Module 1: Basic Economics

Joel Castón

I dedicate this book to my loving mother, Mattie Bell Castón-Foust, who is my Queen. In the spirit of **1 Kings 2:19** I bow before you to give honor to God for your love.

SCOPE

The Currency Catchers Investment Curriculum (CCIC) series for *Beginners* introduces you to the world of investing through the financial markets. The curriculum was created to help anyone who has little to no knowledge about investments.

This course is ideal for those who are looking to learn more about financial investments. The curriculum consists of materials, activities, and content geared towards any person who wants to learn how to generate income through asset ownership.

GENERAL OBJECTIVE

Upon completion of the Currency Catchers Investment Curriculum (CCIC) series for *Beginners*, participants will have basic knowledge and confidence to:

- ✓ Comprehend financial news and periodicals

- ✓ Describe the five asset classes

- ✓ Determine your investment identity

- ✓ Track financial assets

- ✓ Create wealth through investing

TABLE OF CONTENTS

GETTING STARTED

Welcome to the Basic Economic module! A basic understanding of economics is a must to survive in today's society. Financial literacy leads to financial freedom. By taking this course, you are taking the first step towards wealth building.

After completing this module, you will be able to:

- Define economics

- Identify market participants

- Identify the three major markets

- Identify money problems

PRETEST

Test your knowledge about basic economic principles before you begin this module.

1. Which of the following *best* defines economics?

    a. It's the study of money

    b. It's the study of scarcity

    c. It's the study of businesses

2. What creates a market?

    a. Buyers and sellers

    b. Foods and clothes

    c. Governments and citizens

3. List the names of the three major markets

    a. _____

    b. _____

    c. _____

BASIC ECONOMICS

A basic understanding of economics is a must to survive in today's economy. The world is run by economics, and the lack of knowledge about it will leave you behind financially.

Because the world has a limited amount of resources, the administration of the supply and distribution of resources are critical for survival. Hereby, the interaction and exchange among resources are what make the world go around.

Economics is the study of scarcity, or limited resources. In studying economics, the analysis seeks to maximize the output of resources.

The economy of a country or nation can be broken down into societies. A society represents a group of people that forms a community. The economics that govern the resources within a given society is critical for that community's survival.

To help you further understand this concept, consider the fact that the neighborhood or district you live in is a society. It may be considered a society within a larger society.

The economics that governs the resources of your region is vital for your community's survival. To this wise your comprehension on how to survive in your immediate area will help you comprehend the basics of economics.

THE COMMUNITY

A society may be divided into two groups which interact within the economy: people and businesses. People represent homes, individuals and families. Businesses represent firms, companies, organizations, and governments. The interaction within these two groups, homes and firms, keeps the economy afloat.

In order for a community to function, basic necessities like food, clothing, and shelter are supplied and demanded by its residents. The constant supply and distribution of these resources signifies a strong economy. The opposite holds true for a weak economy. Hereby, robust communities are symbolized by an abundant flow of resources.

With this working definition in mind, you are able to rate the strength or the lack of your community. The economy of your household, neighborhood, city, and/or nation will determine the quality of living for the occupants; hence, economic strength equals financial freedom.

THE CREATION OF A MARKET

When people and business interact in the community, they create a market. A market brings together two players: demanders (buyers) and suppliers (sellers). Together buyers and sellers create a market.

For example, a fish market brings together buyers and sellers of fish. A diamond market brings together buyers and sellers of diamonds.

The role you play in a given market will determine whether you are a supplier or demander. It is the interaction between the demanders and suppliers that keeps a market alive and a community vibrant. New products are demanded and supplied over the course of time with the aim to please community members and maximize profits.

This point sheds light on a profound introspective question. Who are you economically? The divide between the affluent and the poor is largely determined by ones interaction in the three major markets, i.e., are you a supplier or demander?

Even though the economy consists of both small and large markets, the overall economy can be grouped into three major markets. Thus, economics studies the interaction of supply and demand in the three major markets.

CURRENCY CHASERS

To survive in the economy people demand jobs for money. This leads to the first major market, the labor market. The labor market represents the sum of all jobs in the economy. Therefore, people supply their labor for employment. When the supply of labor is the only source of income, currency chasing becomes crucial for survival.

In the labor market people are the suppliers and businesses are the demanders. Businesses need workers to produce the products and to deliver the services they supply to customers. The relationship between households and firms in the labor market is based on people receiving payment for supplying labor.

A currency chaser may be a single parent stressing to take care of his/her family in need of a decent paying job. A recent college grad struggling to land steady employment to pay off student loans and simply survive can be a currency chaser. An ordinary person working 9 to 5 can be a currency chaser striving to stay above water. Currency chasers are always in hot pursuit of money.

Have you ever witnessed someone chasing paper in the wind? Picture one of those Hollywood movies. The actress is nicely dressed. She is wearing high heel shoes, and she is walking with her hands filled with paper work and files.

She stops at a vending stand to buy a hotdog and her favorite soda.

Struggling to make the purchase, she frees one hand to make the payment. Smiling, she walks away ready to eat. Suddenly, a strong wind comes along and blows away her papers. Without thinking, she takes off. No time to think about the people in her path; off she goes in hot pursuit of her papers.

In the movies some nice handsome guy always comes along to help the damsel in distress to retrieve her papers. That's Hollywood!

However, many women know firsthand that in real life the knight in shining armor rarely appears. The damsel will remain in distress until she gets her own papers. Do you get the picture?

Life throws unexpected financial storms at the drop of a dime. If you aren't financially secured, an unforeseen bill or expense can blow away your paper (money).

A series of unexpected financial obligations can send you off like Superman or Wonder Woman chasing paper.

Fiscal responsibility consists of budgeting, having an emergency fund in place, saving, and investing to help you weather unpredictable financial outbreaks.

The main problem with currency chasers is that they are stuck in one mode when it comes to making money. Sure some are clever when it comes to making money, but usually it comes down to the same denominator, the supply of labor.

To make a lot of money, currency chasers compete for the highest paying jobs, or they try to find extra work. Some pick up multiple side hustles or jobs. While there's nothing wrong with this, the end result is the same—more labor.

There is only so much human power one can exert. Most people can barely maintain one job, not to mention working overtime. The thought of two or three jobs becomes humanly impossible to sustain for a long period of time. For this reason, physical labor places a cap on the flow of money a currency chaser can receive.

CURRENCY THROWERS

Currency throwing is more common than you may think. For clarity, this doesn't refer to the urban jargon of "making it rain." Believe it or not, businesses throw more money than rappers do in a music video.

In the labor market businesses make it rain.

Firms need workers to produce and/or to provide services. To compensate laborers, firms throw paper to them in the form of wages.

Paper throwing is doable for firms for the paper they throw represents pennies on the dollars they make. When businesses are sitting on stacks of cash, it's easy to throw racks of money on pay day.

It may be reasoned that laborers are paper trash collectors. This language may sound harsh, and yet consider the comparison between the money companies make opposed to laborers' salary. I'm sure that after contemplating you will probably agree.

This point isn't made to discredit the labor market nor the nobility ascribed to a person supplying his or her labor for pay.

Laborers are the backbone of the economy. Nonetheless, laborers must learn to employ *Alternative Money Yields (AMY)* when it comes to finance. The employment of AMY concepts is the purpose of this course.

For years many have thought the risk associated with working for a big corporation was low. However, the collapse of large corporations and job cuts has shattered this myth. Carefully consider the business relationship between firms and laborers. If a company or government is in financial trouble, it's common to downsize by cutting jobs, i.e. workers.

Sometime, work hours are reduced without notice, making the supply of labor a risky business. If you don't believe it, just ask people in the unemployment line.

A heart wrenching reality is that even though the supply of labor is necessary, it can be easily replaced. On the other hand, the supply of money is vital because it is harder to get.

People are quicker to part with their physical labor opposed to the supply of money. For this reason, money suppliers are well rewarded.

The supply of money triumphs the supply of labor. The quicker currency chasers realize this, the faster they will be able to change their financial status.

When money is supplied to a company, the supplier becomes a part owner through stock ownership. A company can also become indebted to the supplier of money through bond ownership.

These relationships give money suppliers sway in a company for money suppliers are indispensable. On the other hand, labor suppliers are dispensable. The former is treated with prestige as co-owners, while the latter is regarded as a mere laborer.

Money suppliers have a seat at the table while labor suppliers are the waiters who bring the food to the table.

As long as labor is being supplied, firms maintain control. Nonetheless, the scales tilt when money is supplied. When you supply both labor and money, you can drink from the fountains of wages and interest. You can have a seat at the table and order your food, for you are not just a worker but you are also a co-owner.

CURRENCY BLOWERS

Currency blowing is a known reality. This leads to the second major market—the goods and services market. The goods and services market represent the overall supply of products and services in the economy.

In the goods and services market people are the demanders and businesses are suppliers. Economic systems are built around communities need for goods and services. People have a high demand for goods and services. As a result, they are willing to part with their hard-earned money in the labor market to buy the things they need and want.

Regardless of the community, currency blowers usually represent the majority of the population. They are people who blow their money as soon as they get it. Just like the wind, they spend their money on every buying urge that blows their way. They are compulsive buyers and addictive spenders.

If you truly desire financial freedom, you must get a grip on your spending habits. It doesn't matter how much money you make, if you spend more money that you make, you will always be in a financial jam.

Currency blowing is a financial disorder that personifies a consumer's mind set. A consumer's mind works overtime to find ways to blow money. The magical appearance of a sale is enough motivation to spend. Even at the risk of going broke, currency blowers spend money they don't have.

Because of their inability to control themselves, currency blowers dig themselves deeper in the hole with credit card debt. Bills in the mail are like letters covered with anthrax, for they reveal how reckless their spending habits have been.

You must ask yourself, "Do I want to make deals or receive them?" Suppliers make deals while demanders seek them. Deals soothe consumers while they are busy blowing money.

Hereby, the most crucial area that needs to be changed is currency blowers' money habits.

MONEY PROBLEMS

What happens when the money that is spent in the goods and service market exceeds the money earned in the labor market? This creates a deficit (debt). The lack of money has led many to use credit cards irresponsibly to make up for the difference.

Even worse, some consumers have been led to take out payday loans at high interest rates and/or they have entered into predatory mortgage loans at the risk of losing their homes.

The thought process of currency blowers is to save or make credit card charges to make purchases. Saving money to make a purchase isn't a bad idea in itself; however, it still promotes a 1:1 ration with the supply of labor being the sole factor. Credit card usage is entirely wrong, for it creates a reverse leverage relationship in favor of borrowers.

Currency blowers must undergo a paradigm shift when it comes to their spending practices. To make purchases currency chasers think about the supply of labor or credit card usage. Conversely, currency catchers think about interest gained on the return-on-investment profits to pay for expenses.

The former thinks about working for money, while the latter thinks about money working for him or her.

Currency catchers think *what can I own that will make me enough money to buy what I need or want?* Emphasis is placed on the supply of money and not the supply of labor. This is the fundamental difference between currency catchers and currency chasers.

Currency throwers (businesses) throw money to currency chasers (laborers) in the labor market. Currency blowers (laborers) blow their money in the goods and services market. The irony is that laborers blow the very money that firms throw them for their labor. They give the money right back! This is a vicious and nonproductive cycle that keeps currency chasing alive.

Money comes in the pockets of people in the labor market and it goes out of their pockets into the accounts of businesses in the goods and services market. This relationship is better known as living from paycheck-to-paycheck. When labor is the only source of income, it can cause adverse money problems.

Sadly, weak economies and community members have allowed money problems to lead them to the underworld for extra cash. Such actions are extremely harmful for the community at large because more money is spent on repairing community damage than community investment.

CURRENCY CHASING CYCLE

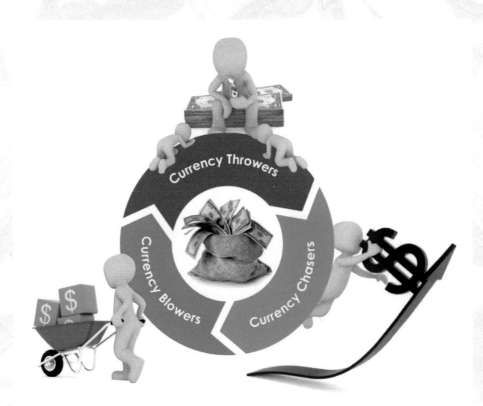

"This is a vicious and nonproductive cycle that keeps currency chasing alive."

THE BLACK MARKET

The black market represents the underworld where all types of illegal activities are conducted. Here fiends are the demanders and hustlers are the suppliers. Because fiends crave illegal products and services, they are willing to pay hustlers inflated prices.

Money comes into the pockets of hustlers and it goes out of the pockets of fiends. Undeniably, the money gained in the black market supersedes the money earned in the labor market. However, the risk doesn't outweigh the reward.

Poor economic conditions of crumbling societies have led some members to the black market. Less affluent communities will be better served by investing a portion of their resources into Alternative Money Yield (AMY) to uplift the community at large.

The financial market is fertile ground to offer employment for less affluent community members.

CURRENCY CATCHERS

To gain financial freedom you must master the art of catching currency and not chasing it. This leads to the third major market—the financial market. The financial market represents all financial transactions in the economy.

In the financial market, people are the suppliers and businesses are the demanders. In exchange for the supply of money, people become owners of financial assets. Asset ownership generates a return-on-investment (R.O.I.). In other words, currency catchers' money works for them.

Currency catching consists of placing yourself in the right position to catch stacks of cash. Money is magnetically attracted to you because you have taken the appropriate measures to align yourself with it. Currency catchers understand that positioning is everything.

Nature has a unique way to express this principle. Consider the strategy bears use to catch salmon. Salmon swim upstream to lay eggs. This isn't a simple task. Not only do they have to fight river currents; they have to avoid being devoured by hungry bears.

Bears have mastered the art of fish catching. They strategically place themselves in the right place to maximize the probability of catching multiple fish. Fish literally leap right into their mouths!

This is the currency catcher's way. Currency catchers position themselves in the place where money is flowing. This increases the likelihood to stack rolls of cash. And, there is no better place in the world to be than the financial market to catch money.

Unlike the labor market, the financial market has its foundation paved with cash. It is the citadel of capitalism and the domicile of wealth. It is the most lucrative place on the planet.

The wealth of nations is stored here. Countries exchange currencies worth trillions of dollars here. Governments offer bonds worth billions of dollars here. Corporations make mergers worth billions of dollars here. Territories conduct import and export transactions worth trillions of dollars here. Billionaires and millionaires park their money here. The financial market is unrivaled!

Financially speaking a 2:1 (two-to-one) ratio is the maximum reward associated with interacting in the three major markets. Money comes in twice through the labor and the financial market.

However, a 2:1 ratio is forfeited when the financial market is left out of the equation. When this is done, you are stuck in a 1:1 ratio which is the equivalent of going nowhere fast.

In order to move ahead, time and resources are well invested in learning how to earn extra money by interacting in the financial market. The math works in your favor.

This is the key to move beyond living from paycheck-to-paycheck. The numbers don't lie. A 2:1 ratio has been a proven business concept for centuries.

CURRENCY FLOW CHART

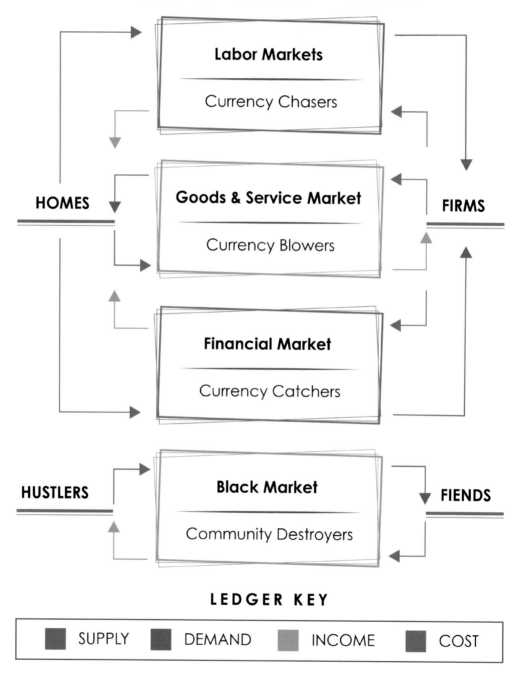

Labor Markets

Currency Chasers

HOMES

Goods & Service Market

Currency Blowers

FIRMS

Financial Market

Currency Catchers

HUSTLERS

Black Market

Community Destroyers

FIENDS

L E D G E R   K E Y

	SUPPLY		DEMAND		INCOME		COST

COMPARE AND CONTRAST

MARKET	RISK	REWARD
LABOR	Unemployment	Employment
GOODS and SERVICES	Damage Goods	Products
FINANCIAL	Loss of Money	Money
BLACK	Loss of Life Loss of Freedom Loss of Money	Tax-Free Money

MORE JOBS, MORE MONEY

More jobs equal more money. In the labor market, laborers work x amount of hours to earn money. This is done until they can physically no longer sustain themselves. However, this problem is solved in the financial market.

In the financial market multiple streams of income can be obtained through asset ownership. Every time money is supplied or invested, a job is created. Your money works for you.

For example, assume you invest $10,000 in an asset. You just created a job. Further, assume you supply another $10,000 in a different asset. You just created another job.

Each time you supply money to own an asset, you create a job for your money. The math works in your favor. More jobs, more money.

Money is the best worker in the world. It never takes a day off or calls in sick. It works 24 hours a day, even on weekends and holidays. It never gets tired and it never complains.

Money is the best worker in the world!

THE TEN PERCENT

Ninety percent of people earn their money from the labor market. However, 10% earn the bulk of their money from the financial market.

That's the secret of the rich and affluent. The rich use their skills to earn money in the financial market. Your training in this course will develop your understanding on how you can also join the 10% club.

ACTIVITY

Fill in the Currency Flow Chart on page 38. Label each object and identify how currency flows from one object to the other. Be careful not to leave out a single detail.

CURRENCY FLOW CHART

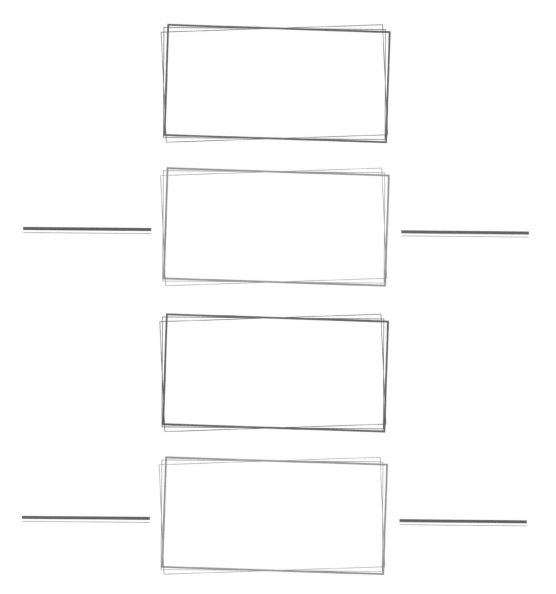

POST-TEST

Now that you have completed this module, test your knowledge.

1. The global economy is made up of which of the following?

    a. Unlimited resources

    b. Limited resources

2. A society can be divided into how many groups?

    a. Three

    b. Five

    c. Two

3. What creates a market?

    a. Foods and clothes

    b. Buyers and sellers

    c. Government and citizens

4. Currency chasers interact in which market?

    a. Labor

    b. Financial

    c. Goods & Services

5. Currency throwers belong to which group?

    a. People

    b. Businesses

6. Which ratio represents the currency chasing cycle?

    a. 1:1

    b. 2:1

7. Which definition best describes money problems?

    a. The supply of labor for money.

    b. Credit debt.

    c. Spending more money than one made.

8. List two risks associated with the black market?

    a. _____

    b. _____

9. Which market does currency catchers interact in?

    a. Labor

    b. Goods & Service

    c. Financial

10. The 10% earn the bulk of their money in the labor market?

    a. True

    b. False

ANSWER KEY

Pre-Test

1. B

2. A

3. Goods and Service Market, Labor Market, Financial Market

ANSWER KEY

Post-Test

1. B

2. C

3. B

4. A

5. B

6. A

7. C

8. Loss of life, loss of liberty

9. C

10. B

CONGRATULATIONS!

You have successfully completed Module 1: Basic Economics.

You can now advance to Module 2: Financial Market.

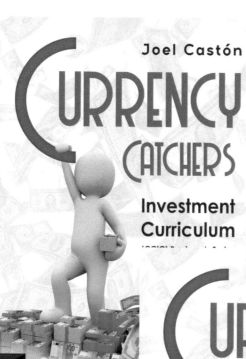

Joel Castón

CURRENCY
CATCHERS

Investment
Curriculum

MODULE 2:
Financial Market

Joel Castón

CURRENCY
CATCHERS

Investment
Curriculum
(CCIC) Beginner's Series

MODULE 3:
Money Mind

Joel Castón

CURRENCY
CATCHERS

Investment
Curriculum
(CCIC) Beginner's Series

MODULE 4:
The BSOFF Assets

MONEY BAG

PLEDGE

THIS IS TO CERTIFY THAT

_____

YOUR NAME

HAS PLEDGED TO DEVOTE TIME AND RESOURCES TO EDUCATE
HIM/HERSELF ABOUT INVESTING IN THE FINANCIAL MARKET.

GIVEN under my hand and
the seal of my word and my bond.

On this _____ day of _____ 20___.

WITNESSED BY: _____

Currency Catchers Investment Curriculum (CCIC)

Financial literacy is the bridge to financial freedom. The Currency Catchers Investment Curriculum (CCIC) educates you about the basics of investing. This curriculum has been designed to highlight the benefits of investing in the financial market versus the supply of labor for income in the labor market.

Upon completion of the CCIC Beginners' series, you will be able to identify your investment identity, cultivate your money mind, and understand the functioning of the BSOFF (Bonds, Stocks, Options, Futures, and FOREX) assets.

JOEL CASTÓN is a retail investor and an avid watcher of CNBC and reader of the Wall Street Journal. He is a Georgetown University student and a founding mentor of the Young Men Emerging (YME) program in Washington, D.C. which is a cutting-edge rehabilitation prison reform system influencing the lives of the 18-25 emerging adults demographic. He is the cofounder of **TRi A·D.** LLC which stands for the three aspects of development whose motto is to change the world from the inside out.

"Easy to read, retain, and apply, The Currency Catchers Investment Curriculum provides a clear pathway to achieving financial literacy and becoming an empowered actor in our ever-evolving economy."
-Aliyah Graves-Brown, Georgetown University Program Coordinator, Prisons and Justice Initiative

"Mr. Joel Caston is one of the most focused and dedicated people in the area of finances that I have ever met. His latest work "Currency Catchers Investment Curriculum" is a good read and I believe it will give readers and participants a good foundation for understanding finances and wealth building. Look forward to great things from Joel in the future!"
- DeWayne Ellis, The Wealth Syndicate LLC

"It is imperative that our community become more financially empowered. This writing takes an in-depth look at several critical aspects and components of finance, the economy and how the relationship with one's finances affect the livelihood of an individual and community."
-Jacqueline McSears Boles, Industrial Bank